Frédéric

Chopin

Eric Michael Summerer

The Rosen Publishing Group's
PowerKids Press™
PRIMARY SOURCE

New York

To Stefanie

Published in 2006 by The Rosen Publishing Group, Inc.
29 East 21st Street, New York, NY 10010

First Edition

Editor: Frances E. Ruffin
Book Design: Michael J. Caroleo
Photo Researcher: Rebecca Anguin-Cohen

Eric "Michaels" Summerer is Music Director and the "morning guy" at the Internet radio station Beethoven.com.

Photo Credits: Cover (Chopin) © Réunion des Musées Nationaux/Art Resource, NY; cover and interior borders (sheet music) Library of Congress, Music Division; pp. 4, 9 (right), 11 (top right), 15 (top right), 19 (right), 20 (right) The Art Archive/Chopin Foundation Warsaw/Dagli Orti (A); pp. 7 (left), 11 (bottom), 16, 20 (left), 23 (bottom) © Erich Lessing/Art Resource, NY; pp. 7 (right), 8 (left), 27 The Art Archive/Chopin birthplace Poland/Dagli Orti (A); pp. 8–9 Berko Fine Paintings/Bridgeman Art Library; pp. 11 (top left), 15 (bottom right) © Scala/Art Resource, NY; p. 12 The Art Archive/Historical Museum Warsaw/Dagli Orti; p. 15 (left) City of Westminster Archive Centre, London, UK/Bridgeman Art Library; p. 19 (left) Bibliotheque Polonaise, Paris/Archives Charmet/Bridgeman Art Library; p. 23 (top left) Frederic Chopin Museum, Warsaw/Roger-Viollet, Paris/Bridgeman Art Library; p. 23 (top right) Private Collection/Archives Charmet/Bridgeman Art Library; p. 24 (left) Hulton Archive/Getty Images; p. 24 (right) Musée de la Ville de Paris/Giraudon/Bridgeman Art Library.

Library of Congress Cataloging-in-Publication Data

Summerer, Eric Michael.
Frédéric Chopin / Eric Michael Summerer.
    p. cm. — (Primary source library of famous composers)
Summary: A biography of the Polish composer who was one of the greatest pianists in history.
Includes bibliographical references (p.   ) and index.
ISBN 1-4042-2769-5 (library binding)
1. Chopin, Frédéric, 1810–1849—Juvenile literature. 2.Composers—Biography—Juvenile literature. [1. Chopin, Frédéric, 1810–1849. 2. Composers.] I. Title. II. Series.
ML3930.C46S8 2005
786.2'092—dc22

2003018674

Manufactured in the United States of America

Contents

Master of the Piano

Frédéric Chopin (shoh-PAN) was a nineteenth-century **composer** and **performer** who loved his homeland. He grew up in Poland, which was a country that had been attacked and occupied by Russia, Germany, and Austria. Although Chopin composed most of his music outside Poland, he was a hero to the Polish people. His music gave them hope that someday they would be free. Chopin lived for only 39 years, but during his lifetime he composed dozens of **classical music** pieces for the **piano**. When Chopin wrote his music he often had memories of his life in Poland and of having to leave his home. He **rarely** performed for large groups of people. Crowds made Chopin nervous. However, when he did perform, **audiences** always wanted to hear more.

This is a daguerreotype of Frédéric Chopin taken a few years before he died. Daguerreotypes are a very early kind of photo.

A Musical Family

Frédéric-François Chopin was born on February 22, 1810, in Zelazowa Wola. This is a town near Warsaw, Poland. His father, Nicholas, had moved to Poland from France when he was only 17. He met Frédéric's mother, Justine, there. When Frédéric and his sisters were born, Nicholas taught French at a private school in Warsaw, the capital city of Poland. Frédéric had three sisters. They played together, ice-skated, and put on plays for the family. The Chopin house was always filled with music. Chopin's mother often played the **harpsichord**, and the children danced. Chopin's older sister Louisa was his first piano teacher. She was seven and he was four when he learned to play the piano. In 1816, Frédéric began taking piano lessons from **pianist** Wojciech Zywny, who used works from Bach and Mozart to teach Chopin.

Chopin was born in this room. It has his mother's harpsichord and Chopin's violin. Inset: This is a picture of Chopin's mother, Justine.

The Piano

Chopin is considered one of the greatest pianists in history. The piano is a musical instrument that is played using a **keyboard**. When one of the keys is pressed, a small hammer strikes one of 88 strings, producing one **note**. The pianist can change how long a note lasts by pressing on a set of pedals with his or her feet. Chopin used the piano's pedals so quickly that people said his legs looked as though they were **vibrating**. The full name of the

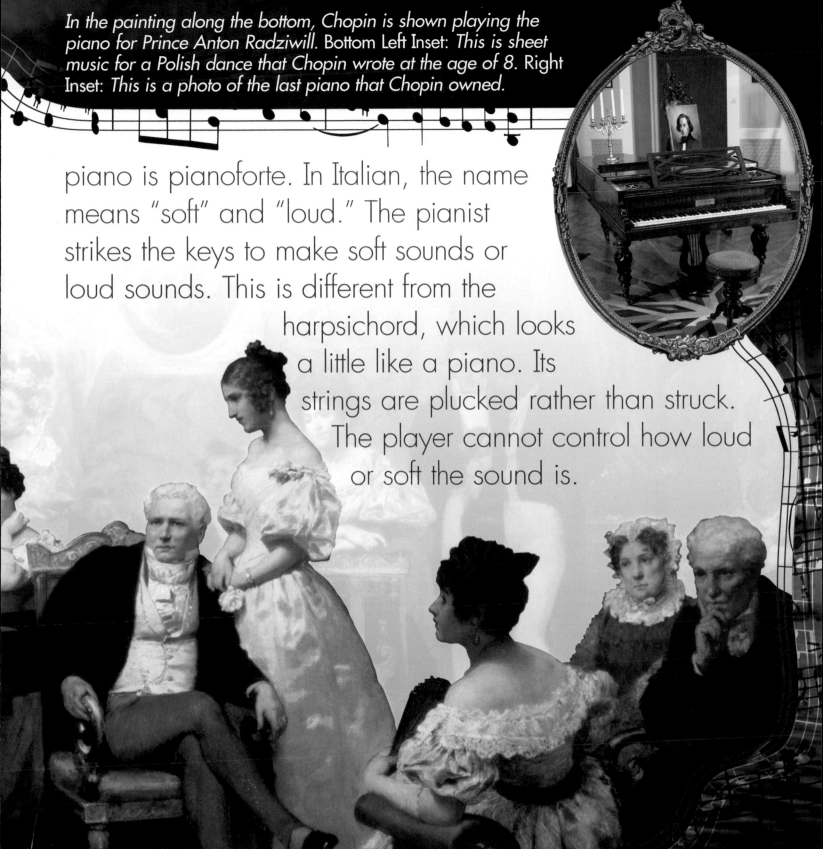

In the painting along the bottom, Chopin is shown playing the piano for Prince Anton Radziwill. Bottom Left Inset: This is sheet music for a Polish dance that Chopin wrote at the age of 8. Right Inset: This is a photo of the last piano that Chopin owned.

piano is pianoforte. In Italian, the name means "soft" and "loud." The pianist strikes the keys to make soft sounds or loud sounds. This is different from the harpsichord, which looks a little like a piano. Its strings are plucked rather than struck. The player cannot control how loud or soft the sound is.

Off to School

As a boy, Chopin liked to play jokes. Sometimes when he played a pretty song very softly, he would then slam his hands down on the keys and wake everybody up with a bang!

Chopin's first public performance was at a **concert** at Radziwill Palace. He was 8. When the composer Robert Schumann heard Chopin play, he said, "Hats off, gentleman—a **genius**!" The little boy was often asked to play the piano at Bruhl Palace in Warsaw. When he was 13, Chopin's parents sent him to the Warsaw Lyceum, the private school where Chopin's father taught. There he studied with the children of princes and counts. Chopin spent so much time around **royalty** that he began to act like a prince himself. He always dressed well, and he never used bad language. After three years at the lyceum, Chopin attended the Warsaw Conservatory, a special school where he could study music and practice playing the piano.

Chopin lived in this Warsaw apartment with his parents. Left Inset: *This is a painting of Robert Schumann, who had called Chopin a genius.* Right Inset: *Chopin attended the Warsaw Lyceum.*

Leaving His Homeland

Chopin's father saved his money to help Frédéric put on a concert in Vienna, Austria, in 1829. Vienna was a great city where many **musicians** and composers started their **careers**. Chopin had such a successful concert that he decided to leave Poland to try to become a famous musician in Vienna.

Chopin left Poland on November 2, 1830. He was 20 years old. His friends gave him a handful of dirt so that he would have a little bit of his homeland to carry with him. Shortly after he arrived in Vienna, he learned that Poland was at war with Russia. Chopin wanted to rush back home to help his friends and family fight for their country. However, his father told him to stay away and to work on his musical career. Chopin never saw his homeland again.

This painting shows troops entering Warsaw, Poland, during the Polish Revolution in 1830. During this revolution Polish patriots fought against Russian rule.

Feelings About Music

People called Chopin the poet of music because he put many of his own **emotions** into his **compositions**. Whenever he heard news from Poland, he wrote music about how he felt. For example, his **Étude** in C Minor, the "**Revolutionary** Étude," was written after he found out that Poland had been captured by the Russian army. He also wrote music that used the sounds and dances of Poland, such as the lively **mazurkas**. However, most of his music was more **sentimental**. The people of Vienna wanted happy dances, like the **waltzes** of composer Johann Strauss. In 1831, Chopin left Vienna for Paris, France. He believed people would enjoy his musical talents in Paris.

Chopin had musical heroes. He loved the music of Mozart and Bach, who had lived and died many years before Chopin was born. Chopin played Bach's music on the piano before every concert.

This man and woman are dancing a mazurka. Top Inset: Mozart (1756–1791) was one of Chopin's favorite composers. Bottom Inset: This is a cover sheet for the four mazurkas that Chopin wrote for the piano.

Quatre Mazurkas
pour
Le Piano
dédiés
à Monsieur le Comte de Perthuis
PAR
FRÉD. CHOPIN

Op. 24.

Friends and Rivals

After he arrived in Paris, Chopin made friends with composers Felix Mendelssohn and Franz Liszt. Liszt was a pianist as well. Even though they were friends, Liszt and Chopin were also **rivals**. Both **competed** for fame in France. Liszt played fast, upbeat music. He waved his hands around and made audiences happy. Chopin's music was much quieter. Although his music was beautiful, his performances did not **excite** crowds as much as Liszt's performances did.

However, Chopin was glad that his concerts were not as popular. He hated playing in front of large groups. Once he wrote to a friend, Titus, saying, "You cannot know, Titus, what a **torture** I find the three days **preceding** a concert." Chopin preferred to play for just a few people, in someone's house.

Hungarian pianist and composer Franz Liszt (1811–1886), shown here, also conducted operas, or plays that are sung to music, written by composers such as Verdi and Wagner.

A Snappy Dresser

Chopin did not hold many big concerts, but he gave music lessons to wealthy princes and countesses. He made a lot of money doing this. He spent most of it on buying clothes and making himself look **attractive**. He wore blue **velvet** coats, silk shirts, and white leather gloves. When he went out, he wore a flowing black **cloak** lined with gray **satin**. He had his own servant, and his own horse and **carriage**. He filled his house with the newest styles of furniture. He always had fresh flowers in his home, especially violets, which were his favorite. Although he dressed well, Chopin did not look healthy. He was pale and thin, weighing less than 100 pounds (45 kg). However, he had a handsome face and a nice smile.

Many foods upset Chopin's stomach. He drank milk but never wine or coffee. He ate only bread, pastry, chicken, and fish. Other foods made him sick.

Chopin is a well-dressed young man in this painting. Inset: Chopin's pocket diary, which he used to write down his thoughts, also held a lock of hair from Maria Wodzinska, a woman whom he loved.

A Woman Named George

Chopin never married, but he came close to doing so a few times. In 1835, he met a pretty girl in Paris named Maria Wodzinska. She was the 16-year-old daughter of a Polish count. Chopin and Maria were engaged for one year. However, Maria's father, who did not like Chopin, made the couple stop seeing each other.

In 1836, Chopin began his longest **relationship**, which was with a **divorced** woman named George Sand. She was a French **novelist** he had met that year. George Sand's real name was Amandine-Aurore-Lucile Dudevant. She used the name George Sand to write many popular books. Sand was six years older than Chopin, and she was the mother of two children.

This is a painting of the writer George Sand. **Bottom Inset:** *Chopin loved Maria Wodzinska, but he could not marry her.*

Chopin's Writing Style

In 1836, Chopin worked so hard that he rarely went outside or saw anyone. Friends thought he had died. A Warsaw newspaper had to print a story telling people that he was okay.

Chopin and Sand spent the winter of 1838 on Majorca, an island near Spain. Chopin was 28 years old. While there Chopin spent most of his time writing music. Chopin spent his summers at Nohant, Sand's country home. He wrote much of his most famous work there. One of the successful pieces that Chopin wrote during the summer of 1842 was the **Polonaise** for Piano in A-flat Major, also known as "Heroic Polonaise." A polonaise is a **ceremonial** Polish dance. Chopin began to suffer from poor health during this time. Sand took care of him. She worried that Chopin was working too hard. When Chopin got a musical idea, he locked himself in his room until he finished writing it down. Once he worked for six weeks on just one page of music.

Chopin and Sand spent the winter in Majorca, Spain, shown here. Top Inset: *This sheet is the first page of Chopin's Four Mazurkas.* Bottom Inset: *Polish people loved dancing the polonaise as shown in this drawing.*

End of an Affair

George Sand grew tired of having to spend much of her time taking care of Chopin. She called him her third child. Chopin did not get along with Sand's young son, Maurice, either. Maurice yelled at Chopin's servants and played jokes on them. Chopin once screamed at the boy during dinner because Maurice tried to take a piece of chicken that Chopin wanted.

The end of Sand and Chopin's love affair came in 1847, when Sand's daughter, Solange, married. Sand wanted her to marry an artist named Jean Clésinger, but Chopin did not think Jean was a very good man. Chopin told Sand that Jean would not make a good husband for Solange. Sand would not listen. Jean and Solange were married anyway. Sand did not invite Chopin to the wedding.

Sand's son, Maurice, shown here, and Chopin were on unfriendly terms.
Inset: This is a portrait of Solange, George Sand's daughter.

A Quiet End

In 1848, Chopin began to run out of money. He was forced to perform more concerts, both in Paris and Great Britain. The concerts in Great Britain were successful, but Chopin grew tired. He did not feel like writing any new music while he was there. Traveling made Chopin ill. He was very ill by the time he returned to Paris after a few months. Chopin died of **tuberculosis** on October 17, 1849. He was only 39 years old. His sister Louisa was at his bedside. His last words were, "Play Mozart in memory of me." There was a huge funeral service in Paris, where an **orchestra** played music by Mozart, as well as Chopin's own "Funeral March Sonata." Chopin's box of Polish soil that he had always carried with him was poured on his grave, so he would have a little piece of his home with him forever.

Chopin died of tuberculosis at the age of 39. This painting shows Chopin with some of his friends before his death.

Chopin Lives On

Although Frédéric Chopin spent almost half of his life outside Poland, his music has become a **symbol** of hope and strength to the Polish people. At the start of **World War II**, the first few notes of Chopin's "Heroic Polonaise" was the last music to be played on Warsaw Radio before the city was taken by **Nazi** troops.

The songs "Till the End of Time" and "I'm Always Chasing Rainbows," are both based on pieces by Chopin. The 1945 film *A Song to Remember* tells the story of Chopin's time with George Sand. The 1991 film *Impromptu* also features the couple. Chopin's music was used throughout the 2002 film *The Pianist*. This film won Oscars, which are Hollywood's top awards for work in movies. More than 150 years later, the poetry and strength of Chopin's music lives on.

Listening to Chopin

Polonaise in A-flat Major ("Heroic Polonaise")
This is one of Chopin's most popular pieces. It is based on
a Polish dance.
Minute Waltz in C-sharp Minor
This piece was written for George Sand's dog. It got its name
because the entire piece can be played in about one minute.
Piano Concerto No. 1 in E Minor
Chopin wrote music for more than just the piano. This is a piece for
an entire orchestra.
Piano Sonata No. 2 in B-flat Minor ("Funeral March Sonata")
This slow, sad piece was played at Chopin's funeral.

Timeline

1810 Frédéric Chopin is born on February 22, in Zelazowa Wola, Poland.
1818 Chopin gives his first concert in Warsaw, Poland, at age eight.
1823 Chopin goes to school at the Warsaw Lyceum.
1826 Chopin studies music at the Warsaw Conservatory.
1829 Chopin makes his first visit to Vienna, Austria.
1830 Chopin leaves Poland for Vienna, never to return.
1836 Chopin meets George Sand.
1842 Chopin composes the "Heroic Polonaise."
1848 Chopin gives his last concert in Paris on February 16.
1849 Frédéric Chopin dies in Paris on October 17, with his sister Louisa by his side.

Musical Terms

audiences (AH-dee-ints-ez) Groups of people who watch or listen to something.

classical music (KLA-sih-kul MYOO-zik) Music in the style of the eighteenth and nineteenth centuries.

composer (kom-POH-zer) A person who writes music.

compositions (kom-puh-ZIH-shunz) Pieces of writing or music.

concert (KON-sert) A public musical performance.

étude (AY-tood) A piece of music written to practice a certain kind of music.

harpsichord (HARP-sih-kord) A keyboard instrument that has strings that are plucked.

keyboard (KEE-bord) A set of keys that are pressed to play an instrument such as a piano or organ.

mazurkas (muh-ZER-kuz) Lively Polish dances.

musicians (myoo-ZIH-shunz) People who write, play, or sing music.

note (NOHT) A tone of a definite pitch, or level of sound.

orchestra (OR-kes-truh) A group of people who play music together.

performer (per-FORM-er) One who gives a play, concert, or other show.

pianist (pee-A-nist) A person who plays the piano.

piano (pee-A-noh) A keyboard instrument with small hammers that strike wire strings.

polonaise (pah-luh-NAYZ) A ceremonial Polish dance.

waltzes (WALTS-ez) Smooth, gliding dances.

Glossary

attractive (uh-TRAK-tiv) Causing people, animals, or things to want to be near you.

careers (kuh-REERZ) Jobs.

carriage (KAR-ij) A wheeled object used to carry people or things.

ceremonial (ser-ih-MOH-nee-ul) Having to do with a ceremony.

cloak (KLOHK) A heavy, blanketlike cloth worn around the shoulders.

competed (kum-PEET-ed) To have opposed someone else in a game or test.

divorced (dih-VORSD) Having to do with someone who ended a marriage legally.

emotions (ih-MOH-shunz) Strong feelings.

excite (ik-SYT) To entertain or arouse.

genius (JEEN-yus) A person of extraordinary talent.

Nazi (NOT-see) Referring to the German army under Adolf Hitler.

novelist (NOV-list) One who writes books of fiction.

preceding (prih-SEE-ding) To have come before.

rarely (RAYR-lee) Uncommonly.

relationship (rih-LAY-shun-ship) A connection, usually with friends and family.

revolutionary (reh-vuh-LOO-shuh-ner-ee) New or very different.

rivals (RY-vulz) People who try to beat others at something.

royalty (ROY-ul-tee) Kings, queens, and their families.

satin (SA-tin) A smooth, glossy fabric.

sentimental (sen-tuh-MEN-tul) Being able to show tender feelings for something.

symbol (SIM-bul) An object or a picture that stands for something else.

torture (TOR-chur) Pain or mental suffering.

tuberculosis (too-ber-kyuh-LOH-sis) An illness that affects the lungs.

velvet (VEL-vet) A soft fabric that is fuzzy on one side and plain on the other side.

vibrating (VY-brayt-ing) Moving back and forth quickly.

World War II (WURLD WOR TOO) A war fought by the United States, Great Britain, France, and the Soviet Union against Germany, Japan, and Italy from 1939 to 1945.

Index

Primary Sources

Cover. Frédéric-François Chopin. Oil painting by Thomas Couture (1815–1879). Chateaux de Versailles.

Page 4. Frédéric Chopin (1849). Taken a few months before Chopin's death. Daguerreotype by the French School. The Chopin Foundation. Warsaw, Poland.

Page 7. Mother of Frédéric Chopin. The Chopin Birthplace. Poland.

Page 8. Chopin playing the piano in Prince Anton Radziwill's salon (1887). Oil painting on canvas by Hendrik Siemiradzki (1843–1902).

Page 8. Inset. Autograph score of the Polka composed by Chopin at age 8. The Chopin Birthplace. Poland.

Page 9. Inset. Last piano belonging to Chopin (during his time in Paris). The Chopin Foundation. Warsaw, Poland.

Page 11. Apartment in which Chopin lived in 1830. On the table is the manuscript of Chopin's Concerto in E Minor. The Chopin Museum. Warsaw, Poland.

Page 11. Left Inset. Portrait of Robert Schumann. Museo Teatrale alla Scala. Milan, Italy.

Page 11. Right Inset. The school in Warsaw where Chopin studied. Engraving from 1800s. The Chopin Foundation. Warsaw, Poland.

Page 12. Troops entering Warsaw during Polish Revolution. Painting from 1800s. Historical Museum. Warsaw, Poland.

Page 15. Celebrated "mazurka d'Extase" danced by M. Perrot and Mlle. Lucile Grahn at Her Majesty's Theatre. Lithograph by John Brandard (1812–1863).

Page 15. Top Inset. Wolfgang Amadeus Mozart. Anonymous. Painting from the 1700s. Civico Museo Bibliografico Musicale Rossini. Bologna, Italy.

Page 15. Bottom Inset. Frontispiece of the first edition of Four Mazurkas for Piano by Chopin. Dedicated to the Count of Perthus. The Chopin Foundation. Warsaw, Poland.

Page 16. Composer Franz Liszt (1811–1886). Painting by Henri Charles Lehmann (1814–1882). Musée de la ville de Paris.

Page 19. Frédéric Chopin. Watercolor painting by Maria Wodzinska, Chopin's fiancée. Bibliotheque Polonaise, Paris.

Page 19. Inset. Pocket diary owned by Chopin (1848). The Chopin Foundation. Warsaw, Poland.

Page 20. Portrait of George Sand (1804–1876). Oil-on-canvas painting by Auguste Charpentier (1813–1880). Musée de la ville de Paris.

Page 20. Inset. Maria Wodzinska. Miniature (1800s). The Chopin Foundation. Warsaw, Poland.

Page 23. Top Inset. Title page of Polonaise. Composed for Wojciech Zywny by his pupil Chopin.

Page 23. Bottom Inset. Pen and ink study for "Les Polonaises de Chopin" (1850) by Antar Teofil Kwiatowski (1809–1891).

Page 24. Inset. Portrait of Solange Dudevant. Done by her husband Jean Clesinger (1814–1883).

Page 24. Right. Portrait of Maurice Sand, son of George Sand. Pastel on paper by Candide Blaize (1795–1855). Musee de la ville de Paris, Carnvalet.

Web Sites

Due to the changing nature of Internet links, PowerKids Press has developed an online list of Web sites related to the subject of this book. This site is updated regularly. Please use this link to access the list:
www.powerkidslinks.com/plfc/chopin/